Old KILKEEL and ANNALONG

by

Alex F. Young, with photographs from the Des Quail collection

John Randall's pub, on the Newry Street corner of Lower Square, Kilkeel, was a popular meeting place in the early 1900s and the place to find casual labour to load granite setts and kerbstones at the harbour. Before Randall, the premises belonged to the licensed grocer Robert Orr. Around 1942 it became Jacob Hall's Central Bar, where the favourite tipple, especially among locally billeted American servicemen, was the whiskey the landlord 'imported' from the Free State.

Alfie Kenmuir, (1879-1964), outside his shop in Kilkeel's Greencastle Street around 1914. The woman in the white blouse, probably an assistant, is unknown, but on the left are his wife Florence, nee Thompson (1883-1926) and their two children; Robert and Florence.

First published in the United Kingdom, 2004,
reprinted 2010, 2013
by Stenlake Publishing Ltd,
01290 551122
www.stenlake.co.uk

ISBN 9781840332780

FURTHER READING

The books listed below were used by the author during his research. None of them are available from Stenlake Publishing. Those interested in finding out more are advised to contact their local bookshop or reference library.

George Henry Bassett, ***County Down 100 Years Ago; A Guide & Directory 1886***, Friar's Bush Press, 1988.
Angelique Day & Patrick McWilliams (eds.), ***Ordnance Survey Memoirs of Ireland, Parishes of County Down 1, 1834–6***, The Institute of Irish Studies, Queen's University, 1990.
R.J. Patterson, ***Catch-My-Pal, A Story of Good Samaritanship***, Hodder and Stoughton, 1912.
P.J. Rankin, ***Historic Buildings in the Mourne Area of South Down***, Ulster Architectural Heritage Society, 1975.
Gloria Wilson, ***More Scottish Fishing Craft***, Fishing News Books, 1968.
Journal of the Mourne Local Studies Group, Vol. 5, 1992.

ACKNOWLEDGEMENTS

The author wishes to thank Alastair Beck; Robin and Gayle Bloomfield of Motueka, New Zealand; Wesley Campbell; Allan Dickson; Albert Hamilton; Bruce Hanna of East Coast Marine Brokers, Napier, New Zealand; Alan Hill; Gregor Holmes; Gordon Hood; Alfie Irvine; Peter Logan; Harry McCalden; Charlie McConville; Maureen McKee; Charlie McKibben; Annie McVeigh; Alexander Newell; Albert Patterson; Thomas Patterson; Seamus Rooney; Stanley Trimble; Alan Wills, Archivist, Gordonstoun School, Scotland; Linda Fitzpatrick of the Scottish Fisheries Museum Trust, Anstruther; the Museum of the Police Service of Northern Ireland, Belfast; Jason Diamond of Banbridge Genealogy Service; and the SELB libraries at Newry and Kilkeel.

INTRODUCTION

Kilkeel

Despite being the Kingdom of Mourne's principal town, taking its name from the fourteenth century St Colman's church, ***cill-caol*** ('church of the narrows'), the surveyor for the 1836 ***Ordnance Survey Memoir*** could only say, 'Kilkeel is a small town . . . containing 103 two-storey houses and 47 one-storey. The former are mostly slated, the latter thatched . . . . There does not appear to be any trade or commerce, except by the country people. It is mostly inhabited by fishermen.' The surveyor could not have realised what the future would bring. By 1846 the town had five streets with about 230 houses, for the greater part well built and comfortable, and a population estimated at 1,270.

But contempt for Kilkeel was nothing new. In 1807 Francis Needham, then the MP for Newry and future first Earl of Kilmorey, attempted, through the influence of John Foster, then Chancellor of the Irish Exchequer, to establish a daily postal service from Rostrevor. Foster was sympathetic, but Lord Clancarty, the Joint Postmaster General, was not. His response was, 'Kilkeel is a small village on the sea coast, [not] possessing trade . . . except what may be derived from the system of smuggling practised there and which is carried on in rather an extensive manner . . . .' No mention is made of the particular commodity being smuggled, but it is likely to have been salt, used in the curing of fish and at that time subject to excise duty.

Lack of a proper harbour forced Kilkeel fishermen to beach their boats on the foreshore and only in the late 1860s was the sand bar breached and a proper harbour and pier built. It attracted more fishermen, but was soon found to be inadequate.

With a government grant of £7,000, to which local interests added a further £3,000, the pier was lengthened and the harbour enlarged in the 1870s – accommodating 21 fishing vessels – but the development was unable to keep pace with the ever-increasing demand. In 1879 there were 1,000 fishing boats working the sea between Ireland and the Isle of Man and at a public meeting in 1880 the harbour master, Thomas Grills, reported that Kilkeel was now the major east coast port, but unable, once again, to handle the demands upon it. In 1885 a further £7,400 was invested and the following year, in his guide to County Down, George Henry Bassett was able to say, 'Kilkeel [on completion of the work then going on] promises to secure a large increase of importance in the near future.' Completed in 1887, this work brought a new wharf and jetty and a deeper basin. There was now accommodation for 100 fishing luggers and during the herring season, June to November, there could be 300 working boats coming and going. In 1890 one third of the herring landed in Ireland passed through Kilkeel. Of increasing importance, coastal traders also brought in coal and carried away granite, oats, timber and, by 1909, 12,000 tons of potatoes per annum. Kilkeel's one major disadvantage was the failure of the railway developers to reach the town and this may be the reason for the high volume of cured herring that was exported in barrels by boat.

Despite the early prognosis of it having no trade or commerce, Kilkeel has prospered. Today, with over 100 boats registered to the port, it is home to over half of Northern Ireland's fishing fleet and sustains a vibrant on-shore industry that includes fish processing, marine engineering and ship repair.

The Kilkeel Development Association, set up in 1991, has identified and corrected economic decline with a budget in excess of £4.05 million. Its projects have included the Nautilus Centre and ancillary tourist projects. The district council's 'Strategic Development Framework: Kilkeel 2015 – Gateway to the Mournes' is also in place and its proposals include an improved link between harbour and town, improved coastal walks, a new hotel and backpackers hostel, a new linking road between Greencastle Street and Newry Road, and another to link the harbour with the A2 at Moor Road.

Annalong

Not being a townland, the name Annalong or Islealong, derived from the Irish Gaelic ***Ath-na-Long*** ('ford of the ships'), does not appear in surviving records until Symington's Survey of 1655. Thereafter, it is mentioned in a census of 1659 as a division of the townland of Moneydarraghmore. By the 1740s, when Walter Harris and Charles Smith were researching their book ***The Antient and Present State of the County of Down***, Annalong was the best of the Mourne coast harbours although, as they pointed out, 'it will not receive any vessel but what are under 20 tons . . .' Until improvements were made to Kilkeel harbour, Annalong was also the principle fishing port on the coast.

In the late eighteenth century, with road building and street improvements going on in mainland Britain, there was a ready market for the easily worked Mourne granite in the form of setts and 'kribbens' or kerbstones. This trade continued into the twentieth century when road-building methods changed to tar macadamized surfaces and concrete kerbs. Today, the skills of local stonemasons are displayed on stone that is imported into the town.

The fishing industry is now based in Kilkeel and granite quarrying a memory, but if population growth is a barometer of prosperity, Annalong, with a six-fold increase since the 1930s, is growing.

Newry Street in the 1930s, with Betty McKnight's draper's on the corner, adjoined by her sweetshop in Greencastle Street. The building was demolished in the early 1970s for road widening. The two-tier granite watering trough (the upper for cattle and horses and the lower for dogs), in the right corner of the photograph, bears the message 'Be Kind and Merciful to all Animals' and was gifted (possibly under the influence of Lady Kilmorey) by the Metropolitan Cattle Trough Association of 70 Victoria Street, London. Founded in 1859, the Metropolitan Free Drinking Fountain Association (later renamed the Metropolitan Drinking Fountain and Cattle Trough Association) gifted over 1,000 such troughs to towns and cities throughout Britain and the Empire. In the 1950s this trough was moved to the junction of the newly developed Knockchree Avenue at Greencastle Street.

Newry Street in the 1950s, with Isobel Montgomery of Ballyardle crossing the junction towards McKnight's. An assistant in McConnel's baby shop in Bridge Street, she later married she later married Joseph Henderson. Her father, 'Old Montgomery', was gardener to the White family at Packlet. On the left, the tailor Francie Cunningham of Harbour Road waits to cross the road. The six-bay Georgian three-storey granite building, extending above Quinn's and McErlane's, has an arched doorway on the first floor due to the fact that, after it was built in 1790, the street level was lowered to lessen the then steep decline into Lower Square.

Children in Greencastle Street around 1914, awaiting the arrival of Halliwell's Circus on its annual visit. This picture was taken at an earlier date than the one on page 4, at a time when McKnight's traded as Hughes & Co.

As Greencastle Street rises from Lower Square, the roadside granite steps decrease until the pavement is level with the road. Sitting to the left of the group on the steps and facing the camera is Barney Curran of Harbour Road.

A Newry Mineral Water Company horse and cart on its deliveries in Greencastle Street around 1911. On the left is McDermott Roe's post office and stationery shop (the post office moved to Newry Street in the 1930s) and Patrick Cunningham's boot and shoemaker's shop that was later bought by Jim Joe Small. On the right the building with the sign at the end of its roof is the restaurant which was run by the McGuiness sisters (who were known as the 'Coffee Dolls') and this is followed by Kenmuir's butcher's, Willie Neil's tailor's, Mrs McGonegal's bakery and Mrs Faherty's pub at the Harbour Street corner.

Greencastle Street, with the Provincial Bank of Ireland (now First Trust Bank) and the trees fronting Mourne Presbyterian Church on the left, and Kilmorey Square to the right. Founded in 1825, the Provincial Bank came to Kilkeel in the 1890s and at the time of this photograph, just prior to the First World War, Mr Samuel F. Anderson was manager.

By the 1920s, when this photograph was taken, the traditional Wednesday market in Kilmorey Square had spilled out onto Greencastle Street and was obviously offering more than the traditional potatoes, oats and live pigs. The market certainly created difficulties for through traffic, but was always a good day for Moore's tearooms, opposite.

A chauffeur-driven Humber motor car at the Kilmorey Arms Hotel on Greencastle Street in the 1920s. The town's other hotels in the 1920s were the Central Temperance Hotel, also in Greencastle Street, the Royal Hotel and the Victoria Temperance Hotel, both in Newcastle Street. The reverse of this photograph bears the caption, 'Edwards family of Yarple [*sic*].' This may be Yarpole in Herefordshire, England, but a search of contemporary records has failed to yield any details about the family.

Local Orangemen parade in Kilmorey Square before marching off along Greencastle Street for the opening of their new hall by Lady Craig on 16 March 1922. In the left foreground is Captain Thomas Richard Chambers JP, who owned the schooners ***Edith*, *William Shepherd*** and ***Harmony***. In his retirement Tommy, as he was known, became a sailmaker. Fifth along from Tommy, in the front row, is the tailor George McVeigh. On the right is the Rev. Alfred Eadie BA, minister to Kilkeel Presbyterian Church from 1911 to 1950. Second from the right end of the first row, to the left of the Rev. Eadie, is the boat builder Harry Mackintosh (1893–1961). The building behind is the Market House and Court House which, although dating from around 1800, is not mentioned in the 1836 ***Ordnance Survey Memoirs*** but appears on the contemporary town plan. Although seemingly the civic centre, the Rural District Council met in the boardroom of the Workhouse on Newry Street. In 1952 the building was demolished to make way for Knockchree Avenue.

Thirty-year-old William Hanna, Worshipful Master, and his deputy, Thomas Richard Chambers, lead the 50-strong contingent from Aughnahoory Lodge No. 343B up Greencastle Street in a parade around 1909. William spent his life farming at 'The Close' or 'Hanna's Close' on the Auchnahoory road and died there on 4 September 1962, aged 84 years. The lodge was founded on 25 October 1861, and its banner shows David, with the Philistines' tents in the background, picking five stones from the brook before facing Goliath. At this time the parade order was Annalong No. 342, Ballyvea No. 343A, and then Auchnahoory, as they headed for Orangeman's Hill on Derryog townland, then owned by Mr Jones Nicholson.

Lower Square in the early 1940s, running into Bridge Street with Henderson's Dining Rooms on the left, the Bridge Bar on the right, and the ivy-covered gables of the old church of St Colman breaking the skyline beyond. The Newry Mineral Water Company lorry, parked to the left, was delivering to Jacob Hall's Central Bar. Established in 1871, the mineral water company's premises on Newry's Downshire Road bottled mineral water, ale, Guinness's stout and Invalid stout. A Kilkeel mineral water manufacturer, T. McKee, appears in Bassett's 1886 guide. Faherty's pub is on the right.

Lower Square, where a group has formed around a cart that possibly contained oysters. On the central horizon is John 'Klondyke' Rooney's newly rebuilt 29-bedroom Royal Hotel in Newcastle Street. Returning with a fortune from the 1890s Yukon Goldrush, Rooney refurbished the hotel and, regardless of expense, installed the latest in acetylene lighting, electric bells, hot and cold baths and six sitting rooms. Destroyed by fire in the 1980s, the derelict building was redeveloped in 2000. Tessie and Nora Clark's 'Confectionery' shop on the right also sold fish and chips. Beyond the wall are the premises of Shannon the builder's merchant (later run by Robert Green) and then the Church of Ireland's Kilmorey National School which was built in the late 1840s and no longer stands.

Breaking the skyline in this 1920s photograph of Bridge Street is the Church of Ireland's Church of Christ the Redeemer on Newry Street, built in 1815 and designed by the Newry architect Thomas Duff (1792–1848). The transept, by the architects Welland and Gillespie, was added in 1885 and the chancel in 1898. The gate on the right of the picture opens into the fifteenth century Church of St Colman, from which Kilkeel, 'Church of the Narrow Place', derives its name. Between 1836 and the late 1940s, St Colman's was used as a school, initially supported by the Kildare Street Society and then Lord Kilmorey. Under his patronage the master was paid £31, to which the Rev. Mr Close, a local churchman, added a further £9.

A Newry Traction Company's engine and trailer making deliveries in Newcastle Street around 1910. On the immediate left is Campbell & Hamilton's draper's and the Orr Brothers' fancy goods shop with their animal feeds premises through the 'Wholesale Stores' entry. John and Robert George Orr's hotel on the right later became the Victoria Temperance Hotel and was a favourite of the civil-engineer-turned-songwriter Percy French (1854–1920) – composer of 'Where the mountains of Mourne . . .' – on his many visits to Kilkeel. The hotel site is now occupied by the offices of the Housing Executive.

Nancy Ryan's Seacliffe House and Tearoom on the Esplanade at Manse Road in the 1920s. The Ryans lived in the left-hand house, which also served as a boarding house, but had her canopied tea tables placed across both gardens. Only in the 1990s were the gardens again divided. Centre of the group is Frank, or Francis, Villiers Ryan, who owned the Lighthouse Tearoom on Cranfield Golf Course. In the late 1920s, while walking the eighth fairway with Sergeant Carton of the RUC, Frank was tragically killed when he was struck on the head by a ball played over the blind approach to the green. Flanking the group are the waitresses Tilly and Rose Cousins, with Nancy Ryan, one of the two women beside Frank. But who was the little girl?

A jaunting car arrives at the medieval fortress at Greencastle. Built in the thirteenth century as an Anglo–Norman stronghold to defend the entrance to Carlingford Lough, it was sacked many times but remained in use until the early seventeenth century.

The first tee on the nine-hole, 32-par, Cranfield Golf Course beside Cranfield Bay. Founded in 1923 – possibly under the influence of Allan Carey of Mourne Grange School – the course was laid out on the farmland of Henry Nicholson of Cranfield (his horse pulled the grass mower!). Membership was one guinea per annum and a derelict cottage was renovated to become the first clubhouse. Its successor, made of corrugated iron and asbestos, later served the WVS at the hospital on Newry Street. Around 1929, shortly after Frank Ryan was killed, the club moved to the present Kilkeel Golf Club course on the Kilmorey estate. In those days a Dunlop 65 golf ball, a type still available, cost three shillings, while a Dunlop Warwick (no longer in use) was two shillings.

Although captioned 'Winnowing among the Mourne mountains above Kilkeel', this 1916 photograph was probably staged to show methods of 'times past' rather than contemporary practises, even on small farms, in South Down. The introduction of reaping and winnowing machinery reduced the time it took to harvest an acre of wheat from around five days for the sickle (it took two and a half days for a scythe) to half a day for the reaper-binder.

This 1880s photograph, by the Belfast photographer Robert J. Welch (1859–1936) (who specialized in outdoor work), is the best-known image of Mourne Park House and its park, lake and boathouse. After becoming heir to the Mourne estate in 1806, Robert Needham, eleventh Viscount Kilmorey, started building this three-bay, two-storey house on the site of an earlier one and additions were made to it throughout the nineteenth and twentieth centuries. Among the Kilmorey papers is a written 'sketch' by one W.E. Russell, who recorded the following: 'The mansion . . . is built of the solid Irish granite for which the Mourne mountains are so remarkable. . . . The scene . . . from the front entrance is indeed very fine. Before you, in the precincts of the mansion is a lake. Beyond the lake, the demesne stretches away with a gently rising slope, which hides the intervening land, till one can fancy that the sea laps the lawn of the park.'

The freshly mown lawns, neat gravel paths and mature trees of the grounds of Mourne Park House. The garden, including two ponds directly in front of the house, was laid out in the 1920s when the main entrance to the house was moved from the south aspect to the west.

Hare coursing at Mourne Park in the 1930s. Claimed as the world's oldest field sport, dating back to early Egypt, modern coursing started at Swaffham, Norfolk, in 1776 and through the nineteenth century spread across Britain and Ireland. Heats consisted of two greyhounds chasing a hare which had an 80-yard start. Lord Kilmorey, one of the earliest exponents in Ireland, set out this course at Mourne Park in 1880. The 'Kilmorey Cup' survives and bears the names: B. O'Kane (publican, Newry), ***Devonia***, February 1883; Earl of Kilmorey, ***Norton***, November 1883; Capt. Archdale, ***Anticipation***, November 1884. The beginnings of greyhound track racing in the 1920s, with a mechanized hare as the quarry, saw the decline of coursing.

The old dock, possibly pictured on a Sunday and filled with tide-bound nickeys and schooners. Perhaps among them were the three recalled in the ditty 'The Peace and Plenty, the Never-can-tell and the Uncle Tom which never did well'. The buildings on the left housed James McKee's grain store and mill. Also to the left is the ***Henrietta***, bought in 1936 by Kurt Hahn and converted to a training ship for pupils at his newly founded Gordonstoun School in Moray, Scotland. The ***Henrietta***'s first voyage in her new role was to the Norwegian fjords, with Tom Newell, who had sailed her from Kilkeel to Hopeman on the Moray Firth, as bos'n and ship's engineer.

With their farlan full of fish, the women get on with the gutting and packing the barrels on the quayside around 1909. The farlan or 'long box' originated on the Shetland Islands where, set out on the foreshore, it was used to cure fish. The women worked in teams of three, two gutters and a packer, and moved from port to port, following the fishing season around the Scottish and Irish coasts. Each of these 37½ gallon barrels held a cran of herring – 700 when at their biggest and up to 1,000 in late season. Before the First World War most barrels were exported to Germany and Russia.

The Bank and the harbour, with the road meandering off to join the Newcastle road on the far horizon. The area left of the road, where granite setts await shipment, is now taken up with commercial buildings, stores and the British Legion Hall. The drama in the television soap ***Coronation Street*** unfolds over Mourne granite setts which were used to build the fictional street. In the basin, the boats running out from right of the horse and cart are Lord Kilmorey's fishing boat ***The Lady Nora***, the first fishing boat in Kilkeel to have an engine, the 1897 Kilkeel-built ***St Patrick*** (N.66), and the St Ives-built ***Water Lily*** (N.385). The large hulk at the top of the harbour was the ***Richard Cobbin***.

The harbour in the 1960s, with Frank Chambers' two-storey whitewashed kippering house on the left, adjacent to the lifeboat station with its arched doorway and slipway into the basin. This was built by Lord Kilmorey, initially to house his boat, ***The Lady Nora***. The boat on the left, N.294, is the 57-ton, 69-feet ***Shalimar***, built at Sandhaven in 1960.

Beached skiffs in the harbour around 1900. At the bottom of the picture is Lord Kilmorey's boathouse and its slipway. The boat in the basin, N.55, is the 1877 Kilkeel-built, 20-ton ***Mary Joseph***, while the one alongside it, with the white deck, is the 22-ton nobby, ***Emu***. The boatyard in the top left was started in 1870 by Cornishman William Paynter, from St Ives, and taken over by John Mackintosh, a Scotsman, around 1883. The building in the centre background, beside the granite blocks, was a salt and herring store, while the building to the right of the photograph was a potato store.

A general view of the harbour in the early 1900s, with fishermen preparing their nets. Beyond them, on the far quay, granite blocks await shipment, while on the left are stacked barrels of cured herring. At this time one third of all Irish herring was landed at Kilkeel. Above the barrels two sailors can be seen on a schooner's mast and yardarm, while on the right a ketch heads out past a newly arrived coal-loaded schooner.

Skiffs in the new dock around the time of the First World War. Throughout the fishing season these boats followed the migrating herring shoals as far south as Waterford. Some skiffs were custom built while others were retired lifeboats. In the foreground boat are Willie McGuinness, sitting on the rail, and Barney Curran (without moustache). On N.123, with its car tyre fenders, is Jim Harry McBride and beyond him is the ***Margaret*** which was owned by his brother Chambers McBride (they were two of five brothers and their father was nicknamed the 'Soft Fellow'). Moored in the top right are three nickeys.

The greatly enlarged and improved harbour in the 1930s with the new channel carrying the Kilkeel river to the sea.

This shipboard photograph, taken on a local seine-netter, shows three of the seven-man crew 'shooting the nets'.

An early twentieth-century diving boat working off Kilkeel, clearing either wreck or debris. The two divers are in their 'dresses' – solid sheet rubber between two layers of tanned twill with an outer vulcanised rubber collar to which the corselet of their helmets was clamped. The helmets would be in the well of the boat. The doubled-wheeled, hand-cranked, diving pump shows two dials, one registering the pressure of the air being delivered, the other showing the depth at which the divers were working. The two readings were interrelated. Although still widely used around the world, Royal Navy training in 'hard hat diving', using these kinds of suits, stopped in 1976.

Greencastle potatoes being loaded from Charlie Campbell's lorries onto a boat, probably Dutch, in the 1930s. Of the workers and supervisors, the following, from left to right, have been identified: in charge of the loading, Tommy Nicholson; George Ewart; Charlie Stevenson; not known; cross-legged and leaning on the lorry, Robbie Speirs; and, also leaning on the lorry, Jimmy Thompson. Opening the bag is Sammy Smith, the inspector from the Ministry of Agriculture for Northern Ireland, 'an important man – who could be full of his own importance'. With him is his son Ewel Smith who later emigrated to Canada, married an Indian squaw and lived on a reservation. In the foreground, wearing the dark suit, is the sailmaker and chandler Tommy Chambers, while leaning on the lorry is Bob Linton – his father, Master Linton, is in the light-coloured suit and soft hat (schoolmasters at that time retained their title for life). On the lorry behind, on the right, are Jim Harry Taggerty and a Mr McCrink, first name unknown.

Bearing the intriguing caption 'Mourne Grange Practice with the Pro – How it Happened', this photograph of the cricket practice nets at Mourne Grange School appeared on a postcard sent on 25 January 1908 by W.F. Harvey to his mother at their home in Northland Road, 'Derry. 'Please send me my belt as soon as you can as it is not here,' he requested. This private school was founded in 1900 by Guernseyman, Allen Sausmarez Carey, who had been tutor to the Kilmorey family, and has long since closed.

Riverside, the upper part of Annalong where the Annalong river is bridged by the Kilkeel to Newcastle road, around 1915. The thatched cottage in the foreground may look romantic and 'olde worlde', but even then this traditional roofing was outmoded. Thatching came in many forms, but in seaside locations such as Annalong the roof timbers had a covering of turf or 'scraws' onto which the thatch of marram grass, cut from the shoreline and with a life of two to three years, was secured. The securing ropes may also have been made of marram. Today, there are an estimated 100 thatched houses in Northern Ireland.

Photographed in the days before 1914, two long cars on the road from Newcastle and on route to Kilkeel stop at Norton & Co.'s Annalong agent J. Gibney. Driving the front car is James Robinson, with a Mr Foster of the Belfast wool merchant, Grainger Smith, beside him. Mrs Magee, the Newcastle fruiterer, sits behind the driver with the Annalong milliner, Mrs Somerville beside her.

Operational until the 1960s, when it was one of the last working water-powered mills in Ireland, Annalong Mill, now in the care of Newry and Mourne District Council, was built around 1800 by Jeremiah Atkinson to supersede the one he built on the Annalong river at Mullartown a few years earlier. According to the 1834 ***Ordnance Survey Memoirs*** the Mullartown Mill, with its 14 feet by 4 feet wheel, suffered due to an insufficiency of water. Annalong Mill passed to Atkinson's son Arthur in 1810 and in 1818 to Arthur's brother, Henry. In 1856 it was bought by Robert McCormick and remained in his family until the 1890s when it passed to his brother-in-law, Abraham Hamilton, and his family. In 1934 it was milling an average of 14½ tons of grain per month, a quantity processed by a modern plant in one and a half hours.

Willie McCartan or 'Old Gusty' as he was known, with his horse and cart at Mullartown Mill on the Annalong River around 1904. His cottage in McCrackens Lane was later a barn, but long since demolished.

A stretch of Main Street, from Caren's shop to the Square, in the early 1920s.

Mrs Linton outside her general store and temperance hotel on the Main Street corner of the Square in the early 1930s. Her assistant and the postman are in the doorway. Adjacent to the right is the post office, run by the McMath family from the 1880s, and then John Gordon & Sons, general merchants. The last house was home to Major Norman Gordon, the quarry owner.

The Square in the late 1920s, when a new car was something of interest. On the left is the post office and John Gordon & Sons' (later Wilkinson's) general store. On the right is M'Birney's chemist's and general store. In the distance, beyond the harbour, the white gabled cottage was home to Robert Gordon, captain of the ketch ***Excel*** which sank in a storm on Tuesday, 12 November 1901, with the loss of all on board. Having sailed from Annalong on the Saturday, loaded with granite for Liverpool, she was forced back into Carlingford Lough on the Sunday and foundered off the Wicklow coast. Also on board were Sam McKibbon, the 33-year-old mate, who left a widow and three children, John Gordon, the captain's son, and an unknown man. McKibbon's body was washed ashore at Ardinavry strand, Wicklow, and following an inquest, where the jury returned a verdict of 'found drowned', was buried at Arklow cemetery. The others were never found.

Looking up Main Street towards Kilkeel Road, the last building on the left was the barracks, built around 1898 and rented by the Royal Irish Constabulary. The local force had a strength of one sergeant and four constables, while the building had one cell. The officer-in-charge in 1921 was Sergeant Michael Martin and the last officer-in-charge when the station closed on 22 February 1965 was Sergeant W.D. Hall. On Kilkeel Road is the Presbyterian Church, built in 1840, perhaps by the architect William Hagerty, and consecrated in 1842 when the congregation moved from Annalong Mill. In 1962, some 40 years after this photograph was taken, a three-storey granite block tower was added to the church and named 'The Rev. Piper Tower' after the Rev. Edwin Piper, who was minister from 1910 until 1945. In 1997 a suite of halls was added to accommodate the activities of the 285-strong congregation.

Shore Road, looking towards the harbour in the summer of 1922, with Charlie Trimble, who died in the 1940s at the grand age of 84 years, passing the time of day with the young ladies. He lived in the last house on the right. The window-gabled cottage on the left was Joe Chambers', and the two-storey house on the corner of Main Street was home to Bob Cousins, the coal and fish merchant.

A 'Kelly' boat (one of the freight-carrying boats owned by John Kelly of Belfast) at the quay in early 1920s. Having arrived with coal, it would have sailed with a load of granite. Behind the foremast is the furled tri-sail that in a 'good shade of wind' would have saved fuel. On the canvas-fronted bridge, below the funnel, the wheel can just be seen.

The harbour in 1955 with the ***Charlotte Chambers*** (N.259) and the ***Green Pastures*** (N.20). Built that year by Herd and MacKenzie at Buckie, north-east Scotland, at a cost of £14,459, the 61-ton, 70-feet-long, Gardner 152-engined ***Green Pastures*** was owned by Victor Chambers. In 1957 Victor sailed her to the Danish fishing port of Skagen to have her fitted with the most modern trawl winch, designed by Andreas Jensen & Son. This new gear, built on top of the hold hatch and worked by the main engine, allowed Victor to pioneer mid-winter trawling. Sold to a new owner in New Zealand in 1965, she was replaced, on 18 September that year, by the 75-feet, Herd & Mackenzie-built ***Green Pastures II*** (N.210) which was fitted with a Casterpillar 380 engine and the newer Jensen Type 85 winch.

Inset: The ***Green Pastures***, berthed at Napier on the east coast of New Zealand's North Island in December 2003, when she was on the market for sale at NZ$170,000 (£65,891). Since leaving Annalong in 1965, she has trawled around New Zealand for snapper, a white-fleshed fish averaging 18 to 20 lbs, and worked around the Chatham Islands, 600 miles or three days sailing south of New Zealand, for the shellfish paua which is marketed for both its meat and its decorative shell. In the early 1990s the vessel underwent a major refit and upgrade, including the installation of a new wheelhouse.

By the right-hand quay, leading along to the mill, are berthed a schooner, a nickey, and a skiff which may have been built by the Annalong boat builder, Duncan Scott.